Who Is Tom Brady?

Who Is
Tom Brady?

by James Buckley Jr.

illustrated by Gregory Copeland

Penguin Workshop

For Gordo . . .—JB

PENGUIN WORKSHOP
An imprint of Penguin Random House LLC, New York

First published in the United States of America by Penguin Workshop,
an imprint of Penguin Random House LLC, New York, 2021

Visit us online at penguinrandomhouse.com.

Library of Congress Control Number: 2021940282

Printed in the United States of America

ISBN 9780593387412 (paperback)   10 9 8 7 6 5 4 3 2 1 WRZL
ISBN 9780593387429 (library binding)   10 9 8 7 6 5 4 3 2 1 WRZL

Contents

Who Is Tom Brady?

Tom Brady looked up at the clock on the stadium scoreboard. He saw that his team, the New England Patriots, had just ninety seconds left in Super Bowl XXXVI (36). He had to lead them down the field to try to win the game, which was tied 17–17. Tom called the play and clapped his hands in the huddle. "Let's go!" he yelled.

Fans in the stands and watching at home cheered as Tom completed a pass to J. R. Redmond. Tom then made four more successful passes. The Patriots got closer and closer to the end zone. Finally, they reached the thirty-yard line. Only seven seconds remained on the clock. Tom then watched nervously from the sidelines as kicker Adam Vinatieri tried a forty-eight-yard field goal. Adam made it! New England won 20–17! Tom and the Patriots were Super Bowl champions! He was also named the game's Most Valuable Player (MVP).

Tom had come a long way to reach that Super Bowl, the first of a record seven that he would go on to win. He had not started playing football until ninth grade. He sat on the bench in both high school and college, waiting for his chance. Even after playing well in college, he had waited impatiently as National Football League (NFL) teams chose six other quarterbacks ahead of him in the NFL Draft. So when he finally got his big chance with the Patriots in 2001, he made the most of it.

Since then, Tom Brady has become the best quarterback in NFL history. He has thrown more touchdown passes than any other player. Tom's seven Super Bowl titles number more than any NFL *team*! He is known as the GOAT—the Greatest of All Time. In more than twenty seasons, he has amazed teammates and opponents, and thrilled fans. He even switched teams at the age of forty-three to win his seventh Super Bowl. From the bench to the top of the sport, Tom has had the greatest career in NFL history.

But how did Tom *become* the GOAT?

CHAPTER 1
Tommy

Thomas Brady Jr. was born August 3, 1977, in San Mateo, California. His family and friends called him Tommy.

Tommy's parents, Tom Sr. and Galynn, both loved sports. His three older sisters were all top athletes. Maureen was a softball pitcher who won 111 games in high school, and would become an All-American player in college. Julie was a college soccer player. Nancy was a high-school softball star.

Tom Sr. encouraged all of his children to compete: "Everything we did—and I mean everything, [even] running home from church— everything was a competition. I guess it made things really fun, at least for the winner."

As the youngest, Tommy lost a lot—and he didn't like it. Once while golfing with his dad, Tommy tossed his club in anger after a bad shot. He was sent to wait in the car while his dad finished playing.

Tommy started playing baseball when he was very young, taking part in T-ball and youth league games. At first, his parents prevented him from playing football because they thought it was too rough. That was okay with Tommy—for a while.

"I loved baseball," he said. "The high school I went to was a good baseball school, but once I started playing football, that's when I started to love it."

As much as Tommy loved football, he didn't play very often as a freshman at Junipero Serra High School. He watched from the bench as his team lost eight of the nine games it played (the other game ended in a tie).

In his second season, he became the team's quarterback because the player in that position decided to quit the team.

Tommy quickly saw that he had to put in some effort to remain the starting quarterback. He began working out even after scheduled football practices. His family would see him for dinner, but then he often left to go to a gym. After not doing well in a footwork training drill called "five dots," he drew his own five dots on his garage floor so he could do the drill at home and improve. He also created a jump-rope workout that his high-school coach later taught to other Serra students.

Even as Tommy tried to outdo his athletic sisters, they were among his biggest supporters. High-school friend and teammate John Kirby remembered, "After every game you'd see the entire family, all his sisters, parents, and even some aunts and uncles. They really stuck together."

On the field, Tommy was starting to show the personality that would eventually help him win Super Bowls. "Whenever he was in the huddle, he always seemed in control," said Kirby. "He never panicked. He was always motivational, not negative."

Tommy threw thirty-three touchdown passes over his final two seasons in high school, and his team won eleven of twenty games. He was rated one of the top six quarterbacks in California. A 1994 TV interviewer said Brady was one of "the names you'll be hearing about for years to come." Tommy was good enough as a catcher on the Serra baseball team that he was drafted by the Montreal Expos! But Tommy decided that football would be his best path to success.

For college, he had a chance to stay near his family by going to the University of California at Berkeley. But the University of Michigan also recruited him to play. Tommy chose to make the journey to Michigan. He knew this would take him away from his close-knit family, but he wanted to prove himself at the sport's top level.

CHAPTER 2
College Star

In the fall of 1995 at the University of Michigan, the player now called Tom found himself waiting on the bench once again.

"There were seven guys on the depth chart when I got there," Tom remembered. A depth chart is the listing of a team's players by position, in the order they would probably get called into games. Tom was number four of those seven.

"I remember being out there the first day of practice and thinking, 'Man, I'm better than those guys,'" he said later. "Of course, I wasn't, but that was always my attitude."

Attitude was not enough. The Michigan Wolverines had so many quarterbacks that Tom took a redshirt season as a freshman. That meant that he could practice with the team, but could not play in games. In 1996, he became a backup to Scott Dreisbach and Brian Griese. The next year, coach Lloyd Carr chose Griese over Tom as the number-one quarterback. Tom was frustrated that he had not been selected for the starting job. He considered leaving Michigan, but he decided to stick it out.

Tom told Carr, "I'm not going to leave. And I'm going to prove to you I'm the best quarterback."

"He had a goal in mind and he was not going to be denied," said Carr.

In 1998, Tom's third season, he once again had to earn the starting position. Michigan had added a younger player named Drew Henson, who was considered one of the best athletes in the country. Tom worked hard and was chosen as the starter over Henson. He led Michigan to a

Drew Henson and Tom Brady at the University of Michigan

10–3 record, and set a new Wolverines record with 214 completed passes.

Even with all of Tom's success that season, Carr decided to split the quarterback job starting in 1999. Tom and Drew would take turns in each game. Drew would start, then Tom would play the second quarter, and so on.

Tom recognized that he would have to find a way to beat eighteen-year-old Drew for playing time. "Drew Henson was . . . a super young player," Tom said later. "Drew was faster than I was, stronger, quicker, more elusive, better arm."

Tom continued to have faith in himself, even as it seemed the coach did not.

"Whenever you talked to [Tom] about the future, he [always said]: 'I'm going to be a starting quarterback in the NFL,'" remembered his roommate Pat Kratus.

In the sixth game of the 1999 season, Drew started and Michigan fell behind by seventeen points. In the second quarter, Tom came in to try to lead a comeback. He nearly did, and after the following game, Carr made Tom the full-time starter—no more taking turns. "Brady really separated himself by the way he played," Carr said. Tom then led the Wolverines to five wins in their next six games.

Tom's final game for Michigan was in the Orange Bowl against the University of Alabama. Michigan trailed by fourteen points in the second half. Tom led his team to two touchdowns and the game was tied, 28–28. In overtime, Tom threw another touchdown pass. When Alabama scored a touchdown but missed an extra point, the game was over, and Michigan won 35–34.

"The Alabama game . . . was as fine a performance at quarterback as anybody ever had," Carr said later. The game's TV announcers called Tom the "Comeback Kid."

After two winning seasons as a college quarterback and earning his degree from Michigan, Tom had high hopes for the next part of his career. But to his surprise, NFL teams did not agree.

CHAPTER 3
From No. 199 to No. 1

Before the NFL Draft in April 2000, Tom took part in workouts to show off his skills for NFL scouts and coaches. Though Tom stood six feet, four inches and weighed more than 220 pounds, the scouts were not impressed with what they saw. As good as Tom had been at Michigan, NFL teams were not seeing the type of skills they wanted in a professional quarterback.

Some of the criticisms about Tom were that he was skinny, and that he got knocked down easily. Many years later, NFL Draft expert Mel Kiper Jr. remembered that out of 576 quarterbacks who were evaluated, Tom was number 576.

Tom still had hope, however. The competitive spirit that he had learned at home and that had carried him through high school and college was still with him. During the NFL Draft that year, Tom and his family gathered around the television waiting for his name to be called.

Round after round went by. Quarterback after quarterback was taken. Tom's name was not called.

"It was hard. It was just a tough day," Tom said. "I remember taking a walk with my dad and mom around the block. They were just so supportive of me."

Finally, in the sixth round (out of seven total), and with the one hundred and ninety-ninth pick, the New England Patriots chose Tom. He was excited to be chosen, of course, but he was still very upset that so many teams had overlooked him.

Tom quickly decided he had to get over his disappointment and work hard for the team. He was so confident in his ability that when he met the Patriots' owner, Robert Kraft, he told him, "I'm the best decision this organization has ever made."

Tom spent his first NFL season as the team's fourth-string quarterback. But he also spent plenty of time learning the Patriots' plays and working with the team's coaches, especially head coach Bill Belichick.

By the start of his second professional season, Tom had moved up to the number-two spot, behind starter Drew Bledsoe. On September 23, 2001, in a game against the New York Jets, Bledsoe was injured when tackled by linebacker Mo Lewis. Tom strapped on his helmet and went into the game. It was the chance he had been waiting for.

The Patriots lost that game, but New England won five of its next seven games. Even after Bledsoe had recovered from his injury, Belichick stuck by Tom as the starter, having seen how good a leader and passer he had become. After a loss to the St. Louis Rams, the Patriots then won the final six games of the regular season. The backup quarterback had led the Patriots to an 11–5 record and the American Football Conference (AFC) East Division championship.

In the playoffs, Tom directed a late drive—
a long series of plays—that ended with a game-
winning field goal for an overtime win over

the Oakland Raiders. After New England then
beat the Pittsburgh Steelers, they earned a spot
in Super Bowl XXXVI (36).

The Patriots faced the Rams, who had beaten them weeks earlier. St. Louis tied the game at 17–17 with just ninety seconds left. Tom rallied his team and again showed why he was the Comeback Kid. Using a series of short passes, he moved the team down the field.

With just seven seconds left, he watched from the sidelines as Adam Vinatieri kicked a field goal that gave the Patriots a 20–17 win. It was the team's first Super Bowl win ever, thanks to the player that NFL teams overlooked until the sixth round of the draft!

Bill Belichick (1952–)

Bill Belichick was born in Tennessee, but grew up in Annapolis, Maryland, where his father was a coach for the US Naval Academy. Belichick often helped his father and learned a lot about coaching.

After college, he took a job as an assistant coach with the Baltimore Colts. In 1979, he joined the coaching staff of the New York Giants. Under head coach Bill Parcells, that team won two Super Bowls, with Belichick directing the team's defense.

In 2000, Belichick was named the head coach of the New England Patriots. Over the next twenty years, he worked hard to help turn the team into one of the most dominant in football history. From 2001 through 2019, his team had a winning record each year. They won at least eleven games in sixteen different seasons. Belichick's total of six Super Bowl championships is the most by a coach in NFL history. His 280 regular-season victories (through 2020) are third all-time, making him one of the most successful coaches in NFL history.

CHAPTER 4
Becoming a Superstar

Tom and the Patriots continued to be contenders in the NFL. In 2003, they won fourteen games. In Super Bowl XXXVIII (38),

Tom once again led the team to the
championship on a game-winning field goal.
He also won his second Super Bowl Most
Valuable Player award.

The following season, the New England Patriots won another fourteen games and the AFC championship. In Super Bowl XXXIX (39), they defeated the Philadelphia Eagles. Tom and the Patriots were only the second team in NFL history to have won three Super Bowls in four seasons.

During this run of success, Tom rarely led the league in any statistics. He still did not have the strongest arm among quarterbacks. He was still slower than most as well. However, he was simply better at the most important job for a quarterback—leading his team to victory. Tom seemed to be able to always call the right play or complete the key pass that led to a score. He rarely threw interceptions (passes caught by the defense). And he inspired his teammates to do their best.

"In Tom's case, his rating isn't stats but wins," said Belichick.

Those closest to Tom saw him continuing to grow as a person. About watching his son become a sports superstar, Tom Sr. said, "I see him being a lot happier and a more contented person." But his father knew that suddenly becoming a celebrity was not easy for Tom.

Tom soon had a family as well as a team. In late 2006, Tom had broken up with his girlfriend, Bridget Moynahan. Then, he met Brazilian model Gisele Bündchen on a blind date. "I knew right away—the first time I saw him," Gisele said. She thought he had the most beautiful smile she had ever seen.

Early in 2007, Bridget told Tom she was pregnant with his child. Their son Jack was born in August of that year.

In 2007, Tom had his best season yet as the Patriots made it back to the Super Bowl. He set an NFL single-season record with fifty touchdown passes. He led the league with 4,806 yards, the most ever in his career. He was also the most accurate passer, completing almost 70 percent of his passes.

The Patriots did not lose a game in the regular season, winning all sixteen games. While the Miami Dolphins had been undefeated in the 1972 season—to that point the only team since the NFL started holding an annual championship game to accomplish the feat— the season had been only fourteen games long then. In Super Bowl XLII (42), the Patriots had a chance to be the first undefeated Super Bowl winner since that Dolphins team. However, they were defeated by the New York Giants 17–14 in a huge upset.

The following season, Tom faced a new challenge. In the first quarter of the first game, he was tackled and suffered a knee injury. He underwent surgery to fix the damage, and he had to miss the entire 2008 season. The Comeback Kid had a new kind of comeback to make.

CHAPTER 5
Coming Back Strong

Tom had to work hard in the 2008 off-season to help his knee heal. He wanted to be ready for the 2009 season.

Working hard was nothing new for him. From his high-school days of evening workouts to his steady work as a pro, Tom knew that he had to keep his body ready for the rough action of the NFL. Patriots teammate Rodney Harrison once tried to beat Tom in arriving first to the team's weight room. He got there at 6:30 in the morning; Tom was already there, and teased Harrison by saying, "Good afternoon!" The next day, Harrison came in at 5:45; Tom had showed up first. Finally, Harrison arrived at 5:30. And Tom was already hard at work. Harrison told him, "I'm not coming in earlier than 5:30!" They both laughed.

While he was training and not playing, Tom made time to plan a wedding with Gisele. They were married first in February 2009 in Santa Monica, California. Then the couple had a second ceremony that summer in Costa Rica, where Gisele had a home.

Tom's recovery from his knee injury was a success, and he returned to the field for the 2009 season. Later that year, he and Gisele had a son named Ben. Three years later, they welcomed daughter Vivian.

After losing in the playoffs in 2009 and 2010, Tom and the Patriots were back in Super Bowl XLVI (46) for the 2011 season. Once again, they were favored to win, but once again the Giants pulled off an upset, beating the Patriots 21–17.

Tom and the Patriots had gone nine seasons without a championship. That streak ended in 2014 and kicked off another series of great seasons. After beating the Indianapolis Colts in the AFC Championship game, they faced the Seattle Seahawks in Super Bowl XLIX (49). New England trailed by ten points entering the final quarter. Tom threw two touchdown passes to take the lead 28–24. The Patriots made a late interception to seal the win.

Not long after that game, Tom and the Patriots were accused of taking some air out of the footballs in the win over the Colts. Having slightly less air in a football can make it easier to grip and pass. But removing air from the balls is against NFL rules. Tom denied breaking any rules. The investigation took more than a year. When it was over, Tom was suspended for the first four games of the 2016 season.

NFL Footballs

Official NFL balls are made from four panels of leather sewn together. A rubber bag inside the leather is filled with air. The pressure of the air is set by NFL rules at 12.5 to 13.5 pounds per square inch. Before each game, NFL officials inspect twenty-four balls from each team for use. During the game, staff on the sidelines swap new balls in and out between plays. At halftime in random games, some of the footballs are measured again to make sure they are still inflated correctly. This rule was added after the Patriots were found to have taken some air out of the game balls in the 2014 Super Bowl.

When Tom returned to the 2016 season, it was business as usual. In Super Bowl LI (51), he set a new record for comebacks. The Patriots trailed the Atlanta Falcons 28–3 in the second half. No team had ever come back to win a Super Bowl game from that many points behind. Tom believed he and his team could be the first. He shouted at his teammates on the sidelines. Video cameras caught him yelling that they had to play tougher and harder and to give it everything they had!

Tom threw two touchdown passes and the Patriots added a field goal to make the score 28–20. He led the team to another touchdown. Then, with a quick pass to Danny Amendola, Tom earned the team the two points it needed to tie the game at 28–28.

That forced the first overtime game in Super Bowl history. New England got the ball first, and Tom drove his team down the field.

At the end of the drive, James White ran into the end zone from two yards. The Patriots had completed the comeback, and Tom had won his fifth Super Bowl—and his fourth Super Bowl MVP trophy! He was even happier when he greeted his mother, Galynn, on the field. She had been sick with cancer and Tom cried as he held her on the field amid the confetti.

Tom's sixth Super Bowl win came two seasons later over the Los Angeles Rams. That gave him more Super Bowl titles than any other player. All nineteen seasons with the Patriots with Tom as starting quarterback had been winning seasons. He was elected to fourteen Pro Bowls, the NFL's all-star game. He was selected as part of the NFL All-Decade teams for the 2000s and the 2010s. But he was not done yet.

CHAPTER 6
A New Beginning

After one more season with the New England Patriots in 2019, Tom decided that it was time to move on. He was looking for a new challenge. When the team did not sign Tom to a new contract, he joined the Tampa Bay Buccaneers.

Each year on the anniversary of his originally being drafted number 199, Tom sends out a note to fans, reminding them of the event. He often lists some of the comments that scouts had written about him back then. He again points out how wrong those scouts had been.

At age forty-three in 2020, Tom was the oldest player in the league. "Football to me is more than just a sport. It has become my life. Every choice that I make is about [football] . . .

what I have for breakfast, how I work out, all of those things. I love the game. I love playing."

The Buccaneers welcomed Tom's skills and his attitude. "If you come here, we'll win the Super Bowl," Tampa Bay coach Bruce Arians told Tom. "You're the missing ingredient. We're a very talented team, but they just don't know it."

However, Tom and the Buccaneers lost five of their first twelve games. The playoffs seemed impossible. But after the team took a week off, Tom's leadership began to show. The offense began to pile up points. The defense got better, too. Tampa Bay won its last four games of the season. They did make the playoffs after all. For his part, Tom threw forty touchdown passes, his most since his record-setting 2007 season.

In the playoffs, Tampa Bay beat Washington, New Orleans, and Green Bay. They earned a spot in Super Bowl LV (55) against the Kansas City Chiefs, who were the defending

NFL champions. Tom threw two first-half touchdowns. He added a third scoring pass in the second half. The Tampa Bay defense shut down the Chiefs' great quarterback, Patrick Mahomes. With a 31–9 victory, Tom earned his seventh Super Bowl championship. He also became the

first player ever with five Super Bowl MVP trophies.

Gisele, Jack, Ben, and Vivian joined Tom on the field after the game for the celebration. Tom Sr. and Galynn, now recovered from cancer, watched from the stands.

After the game, running back Leonard Fournette spoke for all of Tom's teammates through the years. "I'm just blessed to be next to this man. He's the GOAT, the greatest football player to ever play."

Timeline of Tom Brady's Life

1977 — Born in San Mateo, California

1995 — Begins playing at University of Michigan

2000 — After final season in Michigan, selected in the sixth round, number 199 overall, of the NFL Draft by the New England Patriots

2002 — Leads New England Patriots to victory in Super Bowl XXXVI (36) for the 2001 season

2007 — Son Jack, with Bridget Moynahan, is born in August

2009 — Marries Gisele Bündchen in February

— Son Ben is born in December

2012 — Daughter Vivian is born in December

2015 — Leads New England Patriots to Super Bowl XLIX (49) win

2016 — Suspended by NFL for four games for being part of a plan to slightly deflate footballs in a 2014 game

2017 — Guides New England Patriots to the greatest comeback in Super Bowl history, defeating Atlanta Falcons

2020 — Moves from New England Patriots to join Tampa Bay Buccaneers

2021 — Wins fifth Super Bowl MVP trophy and seventh Super Bowl championship when Tampa Bay Buccaneers defeat the Kansas City Chiefs at Super Bowl LV (55) for the 2020 season

Timeline of the World

1976 — The United States celebrates the bicentennial, its two hundredth birthday

1981 — *Columbia* completes the first space shuttle mission

1984 — Apple introduces the Macintosh personal computer

1998 — Leading the Chicago Bulls to their sixth NBA title, Michael Jordan also wins his tenth scoring title and a place among the sport's greatest players

2001 — At sixteen years old, Temba Tsheri becomes the youngest person ever to reach the top of Mount Everest, the world's tallest mountain

2008 — Barack Obama is elected the first Black president of the United States

2013 — Mei Lun and Mei Huan are the first panda cubs born in the United States in twenty-six years

2017 — With her twenty-third Grand Slam tennis championship, Serena Williams sets a new record among all players since "open" tennis began in 1968

2019 — The coronavirus disease called COVID-19 first emerges and spreads around the world in a global pandemic that will kill more than two million people by early 2021

2020 — Lewis Hamilton reaches ninety-five wins and seven season championships in Formula 1 driving, tied for the most in the sport's long history

Bibliography

*Books for young readers

*Anastasio, Dina. ***What Is the Super Bowl?*** New York: Penguin Workshop, 2015.

*Christopher, Matt. ***On the Field with Tom Brady***. New York: Little, Brown and Company, 2018.

*Fredrickson, Kevin. ***Tom Brady (Sports Superstars)***. Minnetonka, MN: Kaleidoscope, 2020.

NFL Films "The Brady 6." 2010. YouTube video, 47:20. https://www.youtube.com/watch?v=05fdhfVrg1I.

*Wetzel, Dan. ***Epic Athletes: Tom Brady***. New York: Henry Holt, 2019.

Website

www.profootballhof.com